EYES OF
DREAMS

LEWIS FIELDS

Dedication

This book is dedicated to my immediate family; and others in my family structure: the Fields, the Wards, the Jenkins, and the Brickles.

I dedicate this book to all the Grassroots social services organizations that serve their communities faithfully. And, to all those non-traditional social workers in the world.

I, especially, want to dedicate this work to my wife for her love and support, for always being there for me.

I want everyone to know that, if they need help, there are individuals out there who are willing to help. Never be afraid to ask for help. Never give up on living life in a positive way and following your dreams!

Acknowledgments

First, I would like to give thanks to God for giving me the vision in writing this book. I thank God for giving me His grace and showing me to have a deep love and compassion for His people.

I give special tribute and honor to Mr. and Mrs. Jones, founder of the Youth in Action Inc of Chester, PA (defunded in 2000).

A special thanks to my high school basketball coach, Mr. E. Beck for encouraging me.

Thank you to the Sonny Hill Basketball program of Philadelphia, PA; Mr. Bill Berry of South Philadelphia; and, of course, Mr. Earl Monroe, former NBA professional basketball player.

Thank you to Giselle Ogando, "creative coach" of Ready Writer Services, LLC.

Introduction

It all started when I was very young, maybe about five years old, that I experienced the gift of love. This intriguing feeling was inherited from my grandmother with whom I lived. The manifestation of this love became my normal, a part of who I was. And, I loved my grandmother deeply. Later, when I moved to Philadelphia, PA with my mother and my siblings; I was able to display the same manifestation of love. I lived on a block filled with kids whom I showed kindness to, and seniors to whom I was always respectful. I took joy in making the little babies laugh and acting like a clown just to make them smile.

It was my passion for showing kindness in community with my personality that prompted me to create the block Olympic games for all the kids in the neighborhood. Although I didn't have male guidance, I would often listen to the older, senior men that lived on the same block. I would sit down beside them as they played checkers, and I'd listen to their conversations. At first, their conversations seemed boring to me, but I found them to be knowledgeable. They talked about the ways of life, they would talk about respect for one another, and the importance of showing good manners. I learned to be a good listener, to behave and listen to my parents. In my case, of course it was my mother. My stepfather never really communicated with me, he had his own biological children with my mother. The seniors on my block had a wealth of knowledge, and I was fortunate to have them share it with me.

Throughout my youth, I shared most of my things with my siblings, my friends, or kids that I knew didn't have much. During my teenage years, I was blessed to live in a time when older young adult Afro American males in the community would proactively engage with teenagers. They wouldn't necessarily talk too much but they'd select us to play with them on different sports teams on the playground. This was their form of communicating and investing in us. And, often, we'd watch the older men play basketball among themselves. There was a lot to learn from them, something I never took for granted.

This is where I found my dream. And, there was one particular college basketball player who had given me my nickname. NBA player, Earl Monroe had become a professional player, later on; but it was because of that nickname that I had discovered what I wanted to become in my life. This insight into my dreams resulted in me becoming a well-known high school basketball player. And, I was able to win a scholarship to college. Something that was not too common where I was from.

Still, today, this is not something that is uncommon for our culture. Although years have passed, there are far too many young people who are a product of the injustice and systemic racism that only, slightly, has progressed in our country. There are still communities that are poverty-stricken, lacking in educational resources, and succumbed to the abuse of those who are meant to serve and protect. But it is my hope that my story will give hope to our people and allow them to dream through the eyes of love and determination. This is why it is my desire for all to know that we matter, our lives matter, our communities matter, and our young people matter. And, when we understand the value that is within us, we can answer the calling that is on us – this is the hope that has helped me keep going in my life.

There were many ups and downs throughout my college career. Still, through all of it, God guided me and allowed me to maintain a warm, caring, and loving heart. I ran into many obstacles, but my heart never became bitter and never gave up. Yet, after 13 years of having dreams of playing professional basketball, something happened to me that would end those dreams permanently. But it was not the end to all my dreams. I could never have guessed the path God would take me on as a new dream was birthed of helping kids find their dreams. *Eyes of Dreams* is my story. A story I wish to share with you about my quest towards my dreams, the realization of my calling, and how I started my life of becoming a non-traditional (unpaid) social worker. As you read my story, I hope that you, too, will be inspired to follow your dreams, never give up, and demonstrate loving-kindness to everyone along the way.

Chapter One

"As far as I can remember, some of my best memories are from when I lived down on my grandparent's farm in Virginia," a mature Lewis Fields mused, smiling from his comfortable chair as the memories came rushing forth. Though he was born in Philadelphia, his mother, Dorothy, sent him to his grandparents' home from the age of one until he was seven years-old to ensure he was cared for while she worked as a live-in made for a wealthy family in Long Island, New York. Spending only one short month, each summer, with him on the farm; his mother promised him that one day she would be taking him back to Philadelphia with her. His grandmother, Mrs. Agnes Ward, spent every moment she had with Lewis, teaching him everything she could; every day on the farm was a thrilling adventure for him filled with new lessons.

While living at the farm Lewis was expected to help with the daily chores, so each morning he made the rounds with his grandmother. Together they fed the many chickens, roosters and pigs living on the farm, and they walked their horse, Charlie, and their cow, Betsy. Charlie and Betsy were little Lewis' best friends on the farm. Other than picking fruit and going fishing for their dinner, his morning walk with his grandmother was the best time he had. After their walk, they would have a hearty breakfast consisting of scrambled eggs, hog brains, fried potatoes; everything was homemade with love.

On the farm they grew everything from grapes and strawberries to cherries and apples; Lewis helped harvest them all. No apple since has ever compared to those apples from his grandparent's farm, they were the best. In his spare time, he would climb to the top of the apple trees and eat the biggest and greenest apple he could find while he relaxed and watched the birds flutter through the branches. Many a time, his grandmother would call for him only to find him in the tree, fast asleep.

As he grew older, Lewis started helping his grandmother in the kitchen more. She didn't have a fancy electric or gas stove like most homes do now. Her stove was a large black wood-burning stove, with large iron plates on the top that she lifted with a small pitchfork so the height of the flames could be checked, adding more logs as needed. "Louie John, don't you go near that stove," his grandmother always admonished for fear that he would get burned. ('Louie John' was always her nickname for him, and he loved hearing her say it.) Of course, one day Lewis got too close and laid his hand on the hot metal plates on top of the stove, receiving a horrible burn; this was the end of him going anywhere near the stove. Instead he chose to help her collect eggs from the hen house and make the rolls for dinner. He would, often, watch as the dough he had helped make would rise from small little pancakes on the steel tray in the windowsill to large round balls of dough ready to go in the oven.

"What was that, how did they rise to be so big?" Lewis would ask his grandmother in amazement.

"These are the dinner rolls," she would say simply with a smile.

"Louie John, would you like a piece of roll?" He thought his grandmother would never ask!

"Yes, Grandma!" Lewis exclaimed.

"Alright then, go and get me some butter," said grandma. So, he hurried off to get some of the butter she had just churned that morning and she slathered a roll with butter and fresh jam. The food his grandmother cooked for him was always the best and nothing could ever compare.

Of all the activities on the farm, by far, his favorite past time on the farm was going to the creek with his grandmother and fishing for their supper. She taught him how to make a fishing pole with a tree branch, a bit of string, a hook and a weight. They would walk to the creek and wade into the muddy water, and fish for hours. One such time, Lewis felt a tug on his line and quickly started pulling it in.

"Grandma! Grandma! I caught a snake!" He cried in excitement as he pulled a long gray creature out of the water.

"That's no snake, that's an eel and we're going to cook it for dinner tonight!" She replied, chuckling. They continued to fish a little while longer and then headed back to the house to prepare dinner. Lewis was so proud of his catch of the day!

Significantly, during his time on the farm, Lewis's grandmother took him on the most rewarding adventure of his young life; she taught him about God's Spirit and the creations of the Earth. He, his grandma, and his grandpa would ride to church every week on the buggy pulled by their horse- Charlie. To young Lewis, that ride felt like twenty miles, but in reality, it was only two.

At night he would stare out into the clear dark sky, struck by the majesty of glistening stars and he wondered about the heavens. He would often ask himself if God lived up in the sky and, at times, would speak to God and ask him how big his house was. After some musing, he realized the sky is everywhere so God's house must be mighty and huge. During the night his grandmother used to talk about God's angels and how they guarded the people of the world, watching over all mankind-spreading love and protecting them from danger. He loved listening to her talk and regale him with stories. Although he doesn't remember all his grandmother said, he does remember her most important lesson: "Be a good, loving person Lewis, and God will protect you throughout your life, forever."

Toward the end of Lewis's time on the farm with his grandparents, he became old enough to start attending the schoolhouse about a half mile down the road. To a child of age seven, the large schoolhouse was daunting at four times the size of a normal house. When he walked in through the large door, he saw the teacher sitting at her desk, facing another fifty or so children sitting at desks of their own. The children were all arranged so that the youngest were at the front and the eldest were at the back.

Not too long after he started going to the schoolhouse, his mother returned from New York and made good on her promise to bring him home to Philadelphia. He remembers this day as the saddest of his life. Leaving his grandmother, whom he was so close to, was the most painful thing he had experienced. He cried for hours as he and his mother rode away from the house, he had called home for the whole seven years of his life.

Chapter Two

Moving from the country to the city was difficult for young Lewis, suddenly he went from living on a quiet and spacious farm to living in loud, busy South Philadelphia. The rowhome he lived in now was vastly smaller than his grandparents' farmhouse. While he now got to see his mother more frequently, his one small constant was that he still did not get to see her every day. During the week his mother continued to work in New York, coming home only during the weekend, this left his two older sisters in charge of raising him.

He, his mother and his two sisters- the oldest named Dorothy like his mother and the youngest named Betty- lived in this routine for three years until his mother found a job in Philadelphia. When his mother found a job as a nurse's aide for West Haven Nursing Home in Philadelphia, he was finally able to meet his younger brother Kenneth, who was born when Lewis was four years old and still living in Virginia with his grandparents. Lewis also met his baby sister, Gail, who was born about a year after he had come home to Philadelphia. His younger siblings had previously been living with Lewis's stepfather. Now, however, both families moved into the same home, making quite the full house with a family of seven and two different fathers involved.

With a house so full it was only a matter of time before the two eldest decided to go live with their father. Lewis however decided to stay with his mother, stepfather and younger siblings. This brought the responsibility of helping care for the younger children on his ten-year-old shoulders, as his older siblings had done for him. Though one look at their round, pudgy baby faces and he knew it was worth it. And so, every morning, as his mom went out to work part-time, he would make sure his younger siblings were fed.

The value of hard work had been instilled in him from working on the farm for so long he decided to find little side jobs to fill his time, as well as to buy treats for his younger siblings and himself. Living in South Philadelphia, Lewis learned how to hustle the right way: with good deeds and honest work. His first hustle was collecting empty soda bottles from the local paper factory. He would pick them up from the factory, take them home, clean off the dust and dirt and take them back to the corner store where the workers bought them. He could collect around twenty at a time and could get two cents for every twelve-ounce bottle and five cents for every quart sized bottle he cleaned and returned.

"Lewis, you didn't buy all these sodas here" The grocer would say to him, eyeing all the bottles in his cart.

"No sir, I didn't. The men from the paper factory bought the sodas and they gave me the bottles to return, that's why I'm bringing them back to your store." He'd reply.

"Okay, well they look nice and clean; how many do you have?"

"I've got about twenty, sir!" And so, Lewis would exchange his bottles for some change and purchase some goodies for him and his siblings to share. He would get bags full of candy, cookies, and sliced pickles. Of course, being the early 1960's, he could get candy for a penny a piece and two cookies for a penny, so he brought home quite the haul.

The idea for his second job occurred to him as he walked the streets of South Philadelphia, just about everyone had white marble steps and a lot of them did not look particularly clean. No one else seemed to notice, or see the opportunity this presented, but he did. So, one Saturday morning, he decided to get himself a bucket, some ajax powder, a scrub brush and a rag. He went door to door, offering to clean the steps for five dollars needing only access to water. As his second job and his first job entailed working for other people, he made sure he did it in excellence.

Being close to Center City, Philadelphia; Lewis often made the trip there and he used to look at the giant stands where men would get their shoes shined. He would watch as men and women would sing songs as they shined the shoes, melting in with the pitter patter beat of the rag against the shoes.

Eventually he managed to collect together his own shoeshine kit and started shining shoes for five dollars a pair. Shoe shining was an art, so he had to not only be good at shining the shoes but entertaining the person whose shoes he was shining, as he did it.

The shopping area of South Philadelphia at the time was called Point Breeze, and they had all different kinds of stores there. There was the library, a doctor's office, a bakery, paper factory, and even a meat store. The meat store was especially interesting because it had live chickens so, when they came in to buy chicken, the butcher would take a chicken, chop its head off in the back, then pluck it and cut the meat up right in front of you. The sounds the chickens made were awful, but there was no denying that it was fresh.

One very hot day Lewis was wandering around Point Breeze, feeling very thirsty. Luckily, this was still in the days where policeman on horseback were common so in the center of town there were troughs full of nice cold water for all of the horses, it was always the coldest water in the city. He was so thirsty that he ran up to the closest trough, smacked the horse that was drinking from it away and took a good long drink from the trough and ran off. The dangers of germs and bacteria weren't as well known then, so he didn't think to be concerned- though he did know enough not to tell his mother of the times he drank from the troughs.

Lewis's mother would always make sure that he and his siblings were dressed well in clean and warm clothes. She taught them how to take care of not only their clothes but themselves, so they could thrive later in life. She would take him and his siblings to the clothing store on Point Breeze Avenue and they would walk through the first floor where all the new items were though, when they were younger, they never purchased anything from this floor.

Instead his mother took them down to the basement of the store where all the clearance items were kept. There was a large box of shoes on sale, usually for about half price, and this is where they would pick their shoes. Oftentimes they would not have a shoe he liked in his size, but he would find a way to make it work. One time they visited, Lewis found a nice pair of brown shoes; the nicest in the box, he felt. He put them on and could immediately tell that they were at least one size too small, but he liked them so much that when his mom asked, "How do those shoes feel?"

He responded instantly, "The shoes feel nice, Mom!"

While curling his toes under to get his foot all the way in the shoe. Those shoes really hurt, and the backs blew out within a month or two of wearing them but at least he looked good in those shiny brown shoes. The display window of the store always had the newest, best looking items. One day, young Lewis was admiring the brand-new shoes in the window, mentioning aloud to himself that the shoes were very nice as he had a habit of speaking to himself. He stood there staring for a few moments when a strange voice spoke from behind him.

"Son, what are you looking at? Some sneakers?" It was two nuns from the St. Charles Church a few blocks away.

"Yes Ma'ams, I was looking at the nice sneakers."

"Are you a good boy, son?" They asked him kindly.

"I ain't bad, I ain't that good but I'm alright," he replied.

"Well you seem like you're a nice boy, would you like those sneakers?"

"Sure! I'd love those sneakers!" He exclaimed as his face brightened. And so, they took him into the store and bought him the shoes he had been admiring.

As they left the store, one of the nuns turned to him and said, "Young man, I want you to continue to be good in your life." He couldn't help but agree after they had been so kind as to buy him the shoes.

"This rosary here is a blessing from us, I want you to say your prayers every night and every morning alright?" The two nuns continued in their counsel.

"Yes Ma'am," Lewis said, and his faith in God was solidified even more that day. He kept going to Gospel Temple, the Baptist church he and his family went to every Sunday. His mother had him baptized at 10 years old, which was a memorable moment for Lewis, though he had forgotten to hold his breath when the preacher immersed him in the water. He continued attending Gospel Temple even through his teenage years.

Lewis with his siblings in South Philadelphia

Chapter 3

As Lewis was growing up in the lively city of Philadelphia, it took him a while to find The Dream, his dream that is. It wasn't until his family finally purchased a television set that he discovered it. You see, as a child; he and his family would gather around their radio during quality family time. On more than one occasion his mother and step-father would have their friends over to listen to a boxing match on the radio and Lewis would get to watch as, after one too many beers were had, Lew's step-father and his friends mimicked the match they were hearing. They usually only meant to shadow box without touching each other, but on at least one or two occasions someone would accidentally get knocked out cold by mistake.

His observations of the type of work the men in his community did never really appealed to him. He didn't want to work at a paper factory, or as a trash collector; and he certainly didn't want to do illegal work like writing numbers for the mob. None of that called to him. For little Lewis, there always had to be something more. One day, as he was baby-sitting his younger brother and sister, he watched a movie that was all about a person of color working hard to become a professional athlete- first succeeding well in track, then becoming a football hero and finally becoming a gold medalist in the Olympics. He sat in front of the television with eyes wide open in awe. This movie had inspired him to become a professional athlete- the only question that remained for him was what sport should he choose?

 As he entered Junior High School, he decided to try as many sports as he could so as to figure out which one was his favorite, which he was best at. First it was baseball, then gymnastics. He truly excelled in gymnastics and by the eighth grade he had made the school gymnastics team and was considered the third most valuable team player by the ninth grade. His best event was the horse altar and he was even invited to compete in the

AAU junior high city championship where he placed second in the horse competition.

Inspired by his success in gymnastics, Lewis decided to develop an event for the neighborhood kids. He called this event the Street Olympics and he thought up all kinds of tournaments to include. There was a Dead Block game, Half Ball Tournament, Fast Ball Tournament, Golf Putting Tournament, 100 Yard Dash, a 10 Lap race where you had the block, a High Jump, Slap Boxing, and even a Hopscotch Tournament; everyone could participate. He got the word out and one Saturday all the kids got together and competed in these games, he even took the time to make certificates for 1st, 2nd, and 3rd place for each event. At the end of the day he handed out all the certificates with a feeling of pride, however when he went out the next morning, he found them all torn up all over the street. He was so disgusted by this show of disrespect that he cried. His little heart was broken as he thought about all the effort that had been put into the event. He couldn't quite wrap his mind around it.

Lewis's neighborhood was certainly unique, every adult made sure to keep an eye on all the neighborhood kids as they played on the streets. So, there was a level of respect between all the kids and every adult in the neighborhood. While his mother was at work, the other adults who happened to be home would keep an eye out for him and report back to her. He made sure to listen to them and not sass them for fear of getting slapped upside the head and then getting in even more trouble from his mother when she got home. This made it very hard, nearly impossible, to get away with anything.

One day Lewis's mother pulled him aside before she went to work. "Lew," She said, "I'm going to put a pot of beans on the stove and I'm going to let them major beans soak with pig tails. Here's what I want you to do: you need to finish cooking them when you come home from school- I already precooked them last night, so I just want you to turn the fryer down low and make sure that you finish cooking the pot."

"Alright Momma, I will." Lewis assured her and when he returned from school that day, he checked on his brother and sister and then turned the stove on low. He twiddled his thumbs a moment before remembering his friends down the block had a game of half ball going on the corner. He loved that game and it was his team's turn for the block championship- he had to go! So, he double checked the stove to make sure it was on as low a heat as possible and ran outside to go play. For those who don't know, half ball is something like baseball but with a ball cut in half and instead of running the bases you hit the ball against the wall of a building. If you hit the ball against the first floor it's considered getting to first base, hitting the second floor is considered getting to second base, hitting the third floor would be considered getting to third base and hitting the ball over the roof is considered a home run. The game was played in teams of two and only had six innings. On his block, instead of using a bat, they used a skinny broom handle.

Anyway, Lewis couldn't wait to start playing! He ran down to the corner and started hitting for his team, and boy was he on fire! He was hitting singles, doubles, triples, he couldn't miss-didn't get struck out once! It was his game to win! About three innings in or so he hears some kids down the block start calling after him.

"Lew! Lew!" They shouted.

"What y'all want? What y'all want!?" He called back, quickly looking away from the game.

"You got smoke comin' from your house!"

"Oh man..." Lewis dropped the bat and ran back to his house as fast as he could! He darted into the kitchen, turning the stove off. The pot of beans and pig tails had started burning and the smell was evident. He put some water in the pot and shrugged as he hoped the water would help. Thinking they'd be okay, he ran back outside to rejoin the game, but just as he reached the corner, he saw his mother charging toward him down the street. They had already told his mother what had happened, it was clear by the look on her face. As soon as she reached him, she smacked him right upside the head, leading him back to the house as she yelled at him.

"So, what happened Lew? You burned the pot, huh?" She chastised, smacking him upside the head a few more times.

"Yeah Momma I burned the pot," He said, knowing he was entirely at fault.

"How you gonna burn the pot? That was the only thing I asked you to do today- don't let those beans burn!" She yelled "I'm going to whip your butt- you know what you're going to get."

This was back when whippings and beatings were commonplace, and parents didn't get into too much trouble for doing it. Lewis was used to getting whipped with a brown extension cord and the welts it caused.

"Aw, man. You're gonna hit me with the extension cord." He groaned, not looking forward to it.

"I'm too tired to whup you now so I owe you two whippings. And I ain't whup you from the day before and Imma whip you for today so when I beat you, Imma beat you three times."

"Oh Lord, Imma get three beatings at one time?" He sighed, and started cleaning out the pot, setting aside the beans and pig tails that weren't burnt for everyone else to eat for dinner while he had to eat the burnt part with only a little bit of the stuff that wasn't burnt. Boy, he never burnt another pot after that and, in a sense, that occurrence served him for good- now he's an excellent cook. He made sure he learned how to properly season things, and exactly how long things needed to cook for and at what temperature. He had plenty of practice too because, as he grew older, he had to cook for his little brother and sister.

Not only did the adults look out for all the kids but the older kids would look out for the younger ones as well. There was an understood system set in place among the kids. They broke everyone up into age-groups and everyone watched out for those in the groups younger than them. When you first started coming out to play you were a pee-wee, then were the juniors, the seniors and finally the 'Old Heads'. These last ones were young adults in the Afro-American community, young men around the ages of 18-24, who would join the younger kids on the playground to play baseball, basketball, half ball and football. While they didn't verbally communicate much during these times, if Lewis paid attention, he could get good tips on how to improve at playing the sports they played. He knew that if he was too fast for them to catch him that meant he was truly fast, he knew that if they said something positive about his game that they truly meant it, he knew that if they teased him about one aspect of his game then he should focus on improving it to better himself as an athlete, and he knew that if he scored against them he was really good. It was a great time for Lewis as a young kid to be able to play and practice with the older kids, especially with his dream of becoming a professional athlete. Guys like Tim, Jimmy, Lawrence, Matt, Abel and more-

they all really helped him on his journey to be a better athlete.

Chapter 4

South Philadelphia in the 1960's, where he lived, was just like a family, although at times it could still be a bit unsafe. There were territorial gangs all over and you had to be from a certain neighborhood or block to traverse certain areas safely. But, that's just the way it was in their Afro-American community, not only did you need to worry about the block gangs, but you also had to worry about the Italian nation, or mob, that they bordered. If you wandered into the Italian part of South Philadelphia, you would have to put up a fight- even if you had friends there like Lewis did. Sometimes during the week, you couldn't leave your territory for fear of getting jumped, though mostly the gangs only warred on Thursdays and Fridays. Unlike today however, they didn't really have guns back then. Instead, they mostly just used knives or their bare fists and box it out. Of course, at that time Philadelphia as a whole was known for the best boxers in the world. Lewis learned quickly how to hold his hands right to guard his chin and temple, how to spin so he could watch his kidneys- otherwise he would have been done.

 While he did learn how to defend himself a bit, when he was younger, he preferred to evade the gangs entirely and became quite adept at it. One of his favorite hiding places was the corner church. He would be getting chased at night and he'd cut right through an alley, make a quick turn or two and head right into the church, and sit in the front rows of the pews before the people chasing him even knew where he went. Of course, even if they had seen him go into the church, they wouldn't have dared to enter it just to chase after him, they respected the church for the sacred space that it was. Though this wasn't the church he was baptized in or went to every Sunday, the congregation knew him well from his escapes into the church.

 In addition to respect for churches, everyone respected family, the neighborhood they lived in, human life, and the elderly. In trying to get away from the gangs Lewis used respect for the elderly to his advantage as well. One day as he rounded a corner, being chased again, he saw a group of elder gentlemen sitting on a bench outside, being a respectful young man and having a good relationship with these people in particular he shouted for them to lift their legs as he approached, running fast enough that the gang members chasing him still had not reached the corner. As the older men raised their legs Lewis slid under the bench, hidden by their legs when they lowered them. He hid there, snickering to himself as his pursuers rounded the corner and passed right by him without a second glance.

 There were a couple times of the week where none of the gangs fought, this was mainly on Friday nights and on Sundays-no gang wars were ever held on Sundays, these were meant to be a peaceful day, a day to go to church and spend with family. Friday nights, however, was the night that all the old heads in the neighborhoods dressed up in their very best and took their ladies out on dates. There would be no fighting on these nights. They would dress in nice slacks, silky wool, gabardine hair clothing, everything in warm but conservative colors- grays, blacks, browns and blues. These were the colors of South Philadelphia at the time. This is just how it was back then- these were the times.

On a hot summer day young Lewis stood on the platform stage of his junior high school, snappily dressed in a two-piece suit ready to receive his certificate for completing junior high. He stood there, smiling in his all black wool blend suit and his black shirt and shiny black shoes with taps on them in the 85-degree summer weather. The moment he stepped off the stage he started ripping his suit off, scratching the itches the sweaty suit had left. Now that he was done junior high school, he was one step closer to achieving his dream, all he had to do now was decide on a sport to pursue during high school.

The whole summer he practiced his gymnastic techniques in the park; doing flips, round offs, back handsprings, and somersaults. He practiced playing basketball, baseball and football as well every chance he got with the old heads. He would go to the fields and watch professional basketball players play and practice, hoping to glean some tips. He watched the first professional outdoor basketball league in Philadelphia play- the Bill Barry League. It was an amazing experience for him, watching the Golden State Warriors and the ABA ball players.

Finally, he had the hard task of figuring out which high school to go to. In South Philadelphia there were three different schools he could go to, South Philadelphia High School, Bartram High School or Bok Vocational-Technical High School; of the three he decided to go to Bok Vocational after his mother's urging. This meant that he was going to a working school; classes started at 7am and didn't end until 3:30pm. They had all their academics in the morning and then their selected trade classes in the afternoon.

His mother bought him four shirts, four pairs of pants, a pair of shoes and a pair of sneakers for high school. These were meant to last a while, until she was able to earn money to buy him some more clothes, so Lewis made sure he took good care of them. He washed them every night and hung them on a line to dry in the cellar, he'd iron them and starch the shirts. He may have overdone the starch a little because they were as hard as rocks- but at least they were clean. He wore just those clothes for about two and a half months, and they stayed pristine.

"Lewie Fields, you've been wearing the same combination about a month now." A girl teased him once, over his small wardrobe.

"Yeah...at least they clean! I've been using KO starch on them- they razor sharp!" He shot back, making all the kids bust out laughing.

With the fall sports season starting in high school, everyone started going out for all the different sports teams the school offered. Football was his best fall sport, so he tried out for the team as a wide receiver/quarterback. He was so excited when he made the JV football team and they put him on the starting line-up, even though he was only about 100-110 pounds. Despite his small stature he was tough as nails and excelled at his position on the team.

The following season was when Lewis really had trouble deciding what sport to go for, both gymnastics and basketball shared the winter season and their practices overlapped. Having already had success with gymnastics, he knew that he needed a new challenge. And, with his success in playing basketball against the kids in his neighborhood, his abilities had improved most in that sport; naturally, Lewis decided to try out for the basketball team. So, as a tenth grader, he walked into the gym for basketball try-outs alongside a bunch of huge eleven and twelfth graders. Not only were these other guys bigger than him, they all had better sneakers than he did. While they all wore the real Converse, he had imitations which made him an outsider there, too. One of the other boys trying out taunted him about taking too many shots, but he kept sinking them. Lewis didn't pay him any mind. Regardless of the opposing factors, he made it through the first day of tryouts, then the second and finally the third day of tryouts!

Lewis had done it; he was now playing for the Bok Tech Wildcats! And, not only did he make the school's basketball team, he made the varsity team; one of just a few tenth graders to achieve this! Two of those few, Earl Donnelly and Mark, were friends of his who had tagged along for the tryouts. While he and Earl were fast friends, it took him a bit to warm up to Mark since he was from North Philly and there was a bit of rivalry between North and South Philly.

Lewis and Mark used to bump head all the time but eventually they warmed up and he gained the friendship of one of Mark's friends, John, as a result. Throughout the season they also made friends with another guy named Al and the five of them became practically inseparable. High school was going great and Lewis was getting to play in more and more games. In fact, his coach- who had played in the NBA with one of the most famous basketball players of all time- decided to start him in the last three games. This really boiled the blood of the eleventh and twelfth graders on the team. They were outraged that a tenth grader was on the starting line-up, and in the last few games which would be the most important. This really made young Lewis feel like he was something special though, he was filled with pride. He was Lew Fields, shooting jump shots from the left corner- a real somebody!

Chapter 5

Lewis's first idol was E. Monroe. While all his friends were obsessing over the other greats of the time like Atlas and Chamberlain, Earl "the Pearl" was the man he looked up to the most because even though he was just a junior in college, he was still playing in the pro-leagues. Lewis and his friends would go down and watch them all play in the Professional Summer League. They would buy sodas for the players during half time and have the chance to say hello to them and maybe chat a moment. It was truly an amazing experience; one that Lewis considers to be the beginning of his basketball career. One day they all decided to get white Converse sneakers, or imitations for Lewis, and write the name and number of their favorite basketball player on them. Lewis of course chose number 10 for Monroe. Oh, how he loved those shoes.

One day when they were outside watching the pros play, when Earl Monroe's friend, Smitty, came up to Lewis and asked him whose name he had on his sneakers. "Earl the Pearl Monroe!" He responded, proudly showing him his sneakers.

"Earl? Yo Earl!" Smitty called, gesturing for Earl to come over to look for himself. "Li'l Lewi has your name on his sneakers!"

Earl jogged up to look and laughed a bit. "Oh man, that's not my name! My name is spelled 'M-O-N-R-O-E'" he said, shaking his head. Lewis looked down at his sneakers and sure enough, he had spelled his idol's name wrong! He had spelled it 'M-O-N-T-R-O-S-E'. He groaned in embarrassment and put his head in his hand.

"We gon' give you a nickname Lewie. We're gonna call you Earl Montrose." Earl said good-naturedly, patting Lewis on the shoulder. With his head lifted high, Lewis was quite proud of the nickname since he had received it from his idol, and it made him smile when the Old Heads in the area called him by it.

One of the things that stood out the most in Lewis' high school experience was his relationship with his uncle, Ray Brickle, who was a legendary West Philadelphia playground basketball player. Growing up, his uncle played with all the professional ball players who lived in Philadelphia- including Lewis's idol: Earl "the Pearl" Monroe. His uncle would take him around to all the playgrounds in Philadelphia to watch him go up against some of the greats, even getting to play a little as he got older. His uncle wanted to toughen him up and make him a little better at the game. It was his uncle Ray who gave him the basketball experience he needed to become a potential college basketball applicant, even though he himself had never gone to college. The experience his uncle gifted him is what fueled his dream of joining the NBA.

The year after he started high school was the year Earl Monroe became the nation's leading scorer in college basketball and was drafted in the NBA in the first round to the Baltimore Bullets. Lewis was amazed! The same man from South Philadelphia he had been getting sodas for, the man whose number Lewis had written on his shoes, the man who was his idol while everyone else fawned over other players; that was the same man who was the best scorer in the entire nation and now playing in the NBA. It gave Lewis hope that, if Earl Monroe could not only make it into the NBA but be one of the best players in the NBA, then maybe he could make it too. Seeing Earl's journey gave him an extra incentive to work even harder to become an even better basketball player. Having already made the varsity basketball team in tenth grade, he soon became the leading scorer at his high school and even made co-captain by the time he finished eleventh grade.

His coach, who had played in the NBA, called in some favors and had some other former NBA players visit with the team, which was a big treat, especially for Lewis. One day, the coach pulled Lewis aside and told him that he was good at playing the game, was a good shooter, was good at listening to his coaching and that he had a heart of gold. Coach continued his praise and positive affirmations, "Lewie, not only are you good at sharing the ball, communicating with others and teaching them how to be better basketball players; but you are also a good friend and teammate to the other players." Lewis felt that had to be his most rewarding achievement in high school; teaching the other guys how to play the game, how to shoot, and most importantly: how to make a way for themselves.

The high school basketball division had six teams participating. Bok Vocational, South Philadelphia High, Overbrook High, West Philadelphia High, and Bartram High were all the schools in the division. There were often times when Lewis felt that their team was the worst because while the other teams would go to the city championships his team didn't. Of course, whenever he looked at the facts, he realized that wasn't the case. After all, he alone had a point average of 21.5 a game and only missed second team all public by two votes and he won an honorable mention twice in 11th and 12th grade in all city.

"Look guys, we might not have one of the best teams in the division, but we're gonna get everyone to fight, we're gonna let them know that Bok is in the building and in the game. We'll share the ball and give everyone the opportunity to make your own name out there." He said in a particularly memorable pep talk to his team one day. Lewis always stressed that he wanted all of them to go to college- even though they were in a trade school and it wasn't expected of them. Still, Lewis always pressed to achieve the unexpected. And, Lewis got his wish too; the whole starting lineup went to college.

Philadelphia's public high school basketball league was full of strong teams in the 1960's and 70's. It was packed with kids who were 6 or 7-foot-tall and kids from West Philadelphia, nicknamed the "speed boys" known for scoring 100 points a game. Edison high school's team won the championship in 1969 without a single person under 6 feet tall. The teams were full of great shooters, great defenders, and no one was a baby about the game. Even when they got fouled by the referee, they took the hit and moved on- no complaints. There were so many kids that it's hard to remember them all now, but Lewis was proud to know that most of the guys had made out well and went to college.

His senior year of high school was when the Sonny Hill league was developed. The league invited the best high school basketball players in Philadelphia to play during the summer. There were six teams in this league - West Philadelphia, South Philadelphia, North Philadelphia, Northeast Philadelphia, Greater Northeast Philadelphia and the Suburbs, each team filled with the absolute best high school basketball players. If you made it onto the Sonny Hill league, everyone knew it was because you were considered one of the best in all Philadelphia. Lewis just made it onto the South Philadelphia team which he attributed to his jump shot. This was no small feat; the Sonny Hill League provided a huge opportunity to showcase the greatest high school basketball players in South Philadelphia. To Lewis, being a part of the league was one of his most inspirational moments. Mr. Hill also got some professional athletes involved in the league, giving the kids a chance to interact with them, which motivated them all the more.

That very first year he got to play all over the city wearing a special Sonny Hill shirt that Mr. Hill had ordered for everyone. That shirt earned him a little bit of respect; it was a special honor. Wearing that shirt said to anyone who saw him in it that he was one of the best high school basketball players in all of Philadelphia. None of the gangs bothered him, no one started any fights, no one would dare - it was a good time. At the end of the season, all of Lewis's hard work came to fruition when he and his team won the first Sonny Hill high school competition. What an experience! He ended up missing the Senior Ball to go on to the four-city basketball tournament held in New Jersey. He may have missed the opportunity to go to the big dance, but he also made a bunch of friends from all over and gained the opportunity of being one step closer to his dream. Now, this was the first time he played against a Catholic school basketball team, and he enjoyed the experience of befriending people of not only another religion, but also another race at a time when it wasn't necessarily common.

Sacrificing some high school events was worth the long-term gain for the players in the Sonny Hill League because it opened up opportunities to develop friendships and allowed them to go further than they would have imagined in those days. Players like K. Washington who ended up attending Temple University and M. Howard who was accepted into the University of Maryland. Lewis had another friend, McCarter, who went on to attend UCLA. It was their hard work and the spotlight of being considered the best in South Philly through the league, that allowed all of these young men to move on in their academic careers and into colleges.

Participating in the league's four-city tournament was a marvelous send off for Lewis as he moved on from high school and went to Northwest Community college in Wyoming on a basketball scholarship with aspirations to get to the University of Wyoming the next year. Every experience Lewis had served a purpose; and, for that, he was truly grateful.

Lewis' High School graduation picture

Chapter 6

Lewis's adventures in College Basketball started with a letter of intent from Northwest Community College stating he had won a scholarship. The letter of intent stated he would start at the junior college and then move on to division one at the state college after one year if his grades were good. He brought the letter home to his mother, proudly calling out for her.

"Ay Mom!! Mom!! I won a scholarship to play basketball out in Wyoming!" He said as he found her.

"Oh yeah?"

"See?! You remember, you never came to see me play at all."

"Lew, I heard you can play ball...that what you saying out in the neighborhood?"

"Yeah, I can play a little bit mom, you know I'm trying to go to college." Lew, modestly, replied to his mom.

"Ah, you not gonna go to college, Lew. You go ahead and sign up for the army and if you don't go to the army you going to go down to work at the trash company. I know somebody down there. They can get you a job"

"Ay Mom. I'm going to college." Lewis was determined, he wouldn't let anything stop him. "You'll see and by the way Momma I have a letter you need to sign. It says that you're allowing me to take that basketball scholarship to go to college." He said, holding it out.

"Boy I ain't signing my name on no paper. You're just trying to mess up my rent. Talkin' about this college stuff. Mess up my rent with the Jew man down there. I ain't signing my name on nothing like that, I don't know what it is. I'm not signing one bit." She said, looking at Lewis and then to the paper in his hand, shaking her head.

"Mom! Please! This is for me to go to college." He tried again, pleading a little and, now, holding the letter in both hands.

"I ain't signing no paper; what I tell ya." His mother would not concede, her tone holding no more room for discussion on the matter.

Now, Lewis' family roots came from the countryside. Many of the older generations hadn't graduated from high school. The idea of going to college was not something the family thought about and it certainly wasn't a topic of discussion around the dinner table. For his family, working or serving in the military were the only options. As his mother continued, Lewis thought back to all the times he would talk about basketball and his mother's frequent reply, "There he goes, dreaming again."

Lewis sighed in defeat as he looked at her, realizing there was no way he would get her signature on that paper. He dropped his head, looked down at the letter in his hands, and headed outside. All that he had worked for, all his practice, all his words of encouragement for his team members who would get to attend college. How could Lewis not go to college, too? After a moment's thought he found a pen, stared at it for a while, and finally forged his mother's signature and left to give it to his coach.

He spent the whole summer practicing basketball and working at a local restaurant, Minute Chef. He worked there as a dishwasher, trying to save up as much money as he could. He needed to save as much money as possible to get clothes and other necessities for the Fall semester. He bought a big black locker suitcase and slowly filled it with clothes, sneakers, shoes and everything he needed for college. He did this repeatedly and secretly since his mother had no idea of Lewis' plan. Around August he was ready to go off on the adventure of a lifetime, fulfilling his dreams. When the day finally came for him to travel from his home in South Philadelphia to the college in Wyoming, he dragged his big black trunk down the steps, his mother stopping him at the bottom.

"Where you goin' Lew?" She said, eyeing the luggage and then him.

"Mom, I'm going to the airport because I'm going to college." He explained.

"You goin' where?" His mother asked skeptically, walking up the stairs towards him and crossing her arms.

"Mom, I'm going to college! I told you I won a scholarship, but you ain't believe me."

"Now listen here. If you leave this house with that suitcase don't you never come back again. I told you about that. If you run away from here, don't you come back here no more. If you leave this house, don't come back." She said sternly, shaking a finger at him in anger.

"Momma, I'm going to college because I'm on a basketball scholarship. I'm goin' and I'm gonna get a hack." He tried explaining again. Back then, a hack was an unlicensed cab driver or courtesy drivers who commonly drove in working-class neighborhoods.

"Here you go again fantasizing." She said, shaking her head, still refusing to believe him.

"Look, when I come back with the hack, you can take a ride with me to the airport if you don't believe me." Lewis tried once more.

"Well alright then, I'll see you when you come back."

Lewis nodded and went to get the hack (unlicensed cab) and then came back inside. "Alright Mom, you want to go with me?"

"Yeah, I want to see where you're going." She said, so she followed him back outside and they took the hack to the airport. When they pulled up to the airport and Lew's mom saw his plane ticket in hand, she turned to Lewis, finally starting to believe.

"Mom, I'm really going." Lewis looked back at his mom solemnly.

"You're...really going?"

"Yeah, I'm really going." He said proudly. They walked up to the gate for the plane he was getting on and he handed over his tickets. As he started to enter the plane, he turned back one final time to look at his mother, finding that she had tears streaming down her face.

"Momma, Imma be alright. I'm going to college, Imma make it into the NBA and Imma buy you a house someday." He promised her. As he boarded the plane, tears started falling down his cheeks. This was the saddest moment of Lewis' life.

Seeing his mother cry was too much for him, so as the plane rose through the clouds above Philadelphia a sadness settled in his heart as he left her behind. Lewis had traveled from Virginia to Philadelphia, and anywhere they went would always be by car. This would, not only be Lewis' saddest moment and time away from home, but also his first plane ride ever. And, this plane ride seemed to drag on, taking what felt like half a day before finally sinking back down below the clouds. This was the longest ride he'd ever had in his life. Lewis looked out of the window toward the ground, watching the landing strip grow closer. As the plane grew closer to the runway, he could see that it was built into a mountain, the runway being the highest point with the buildings surrounding it about a half mile down.

"Excuse me Miss? Where are we?" He asked, getting the flight attendant's attention.

"We're landing in the Billings, Montana airport." She replied.

"Montana? I only heard about Montana on TV. I ain't never seen no cowboys or anything live, I only seen them on TV." He said, somewhat amazed. "This is something like a culture shock." He chuckled, watching the descent through the window. As he was leaving the plane at the terminal, he caught sight of snowflakes falling gently from the sky. "Snow? In August?" Lewis marveled at the strange sight in front of him for a moment before stepping off the plane.

Upon his arrival he was greeted by the head basketball coach, Mr. Cabre, who also had attended the four-city tournament in New Jersey which Lewis had competed in.

"Welcome to Montana, Lew! As you know our school is located in Wyoming, but this was the closest airport. We're about fifty miles from the school right now. It's a small college, we only have about 2,500 students. But I think you'll like it." Mr. Cabre said welcomingly, shaking his hand.

"I don't even know what to say coach, thank you for having me! I'll do the best I can for the team!" Lewis promised with excitement for the future brightening his voice. They gathered his luggage from the baggage claim, and they got on the bus headed to the college.

The bus ride was long, leading through wide open fields as far as the eye could see. As the bus drove the many miles, the sky was a deep bright blue. Lewis had never seen anything like this before. He felt transported to a different world when they finally entered the small cowboy town of Powell, Wyoming. There, he didn't know what to expect.

SWEET LEW

LEW FIELDS SHOOTS FOR THE HOOP DURING A 1970 GAME. (POWELL TRIBUNE PHOTO)

...rs were expected to be renewed ...nufactors in the tourney. With ...largest crowd in tournament his... ...y for a non-title game, the Blue ...gers (21-3) opened up an 11-2 ...d early and a 37-30 half-time ...d before setting the tournament ...rd for most points scored by a

...coupled with nine from Gaffi... eight from Childress and sev... from Rogers, but trailed, 43-33 the half.

Gibbs blew it open with 15 in... second half — including and 9-... 10 performance in the free-thr... line in foals, sent the scorer of...

Chapter 7

Mr. Cabre gave Lewis and the other basketball players that were on the bus with him a tour around the college which, for Lewis, ended at the dorm room that would be his home for the time being. Later in the evening, he met the rest of his 12-man team, soon learning that he and four others were the only African Americans in the city. This meant most people stared when he and his fellow African Americans were around, though he was quick to get used to it. The city was fairly small with a population of only 2-3 thousand people, most of whom were Caucasian, and the remaining portion were Native American. But it was basketball that brought everyone together. The sport erased skin color, race, and religion. This made it easy to adapt to the culture. The only other sport the college really focused on were rodeo sports. This was the first time Lewis had ever even heard of the rodeo, it certainly wasn't on anything he had watched on TV. So, seeing all the people in cowboy hats and boots was certainly a new experience.

After having met the rest of his Trappers teammates, he felt more at home knowing he wasn't the only one new to this environment and that they would all have basketball in common. As the days went on and they started practicing more and more together, they really pulled together as a team. Before Lewis knew it, he was moved to a starting lineup position on the team and this motivated him to try even harder at improving not only his game, but also his grades to ensure he didn't lose his scholarship. This earned him a respectable 2.7 grade point average in his Business Administration major. More impressive than his GPA was his game average which was in the double digits with two to three steals and three to four assists per game. Oh, it was a thrill to play for the crowd. Lewis loved to entertain the basketball fans that would pack out the gym.

Lewis had quite a few adventures during his time in Wyoming. For instance, one day he was in the cafeteria for lunch and he sat down with his teammates, digging into the beef, mashed potatoes with gravy and vegetables they were serving that day. "Boy this beef sure is good today!" He said happily enjoying the portion that was already in his mouth.

"You don't know what you're eating, do you?" One of his teammates chuckled, looking at what Lewis had on his plate.

"Yeah, I do. It's beef, right?" Lewis replied.

"Technically... Those are calf balls."

"What...Calf balls?!" Lewis's eyes grew wide and he hopped up from the table, running to the bathroom unable to keep his lunch down now that he knew what it really was.

Then, on another occasion, he was out hunting for rabbits in the Grand Canyon with some friends, a good time with friends in a beautiful place. What could be better?

"You know what you should look for, Lew?" One of his cowboy friends asked as they wandered around. "You need to look for a jackalope. If you find one of those you can get a lot of money for 'em. That's where the big hunting money is."

"What's a jackalope?" He asked.

"It's a king-sized rabbit with antlers like a deer." His friend explained helpfully.

Lewis nodded, "Alright, good to know." And, he started looking around for a jackalope. He spent hours and hours searching, determined to find it for the big hunt. But when their daytrip was finally over, Lewis met back up with everyone, exhausted and without a single kill.

"Man, I couldn't find no jackalope." He said to one of his friends, shaking his head as he looked around at all of his friends' many kills. As soon as the words left his mouth everyone else started laughing hysterically, much to his confusion.

"Lew…. There's no such thing as a jackalope man, it's a myth! It ain't real." They choked out between laughs.

"Aw man, this was a joke?!" He groaned utterly.

"Yeah man, we didn't think you'd fall for it," they said, still laughing.

"Alright, alright; the joke is on me guys." He sighed. He couldn't believe how gullible he had been but still enjoyed the time with friends.

Lewis's major in college was recreation with a minor in sociology and urban studies. He wasn't sure what profession he was going into with this degree, he just knew he wanted to play in the NBA. That was the only thing he was sure of, no matter where he went, state to state, college to college, his only and main goal was play professional basketball.

Overall, everything was going as Lewis had planned. But of all the changes and difficulties he had to face leaving his home, living the dorm life was the most difficult. Playing harmless pranks among friends was one thing, but there was a small group of guys in the dorms that took the horseplay too far. They would constantly place traps inside the dorm rooms of the other students, often ruining their belongings.

One night, this group of pranksters placed a trash can, filled to the brim with water, behind Lewis' door. When Lewis came back to his room and opened the door, the trash bin toppled over and flooded his room. All of his stuff was soaking wet and Lewis was furious! Lew went to his friends and teammates to tell them what had happened which escalated to a large fight.

The next morning, Lew was called into the academic director's office. Someone had accused him of starting the whole thing. His coach approached Lewis in the hall and bore the bad news.

"Lew, we have to expel you from school."

"What? Coach, why?" In complete disbelief, Lew appealed.

"I'm not sure, Lew. But I believe one of the boys you fought, well his father sits on the disciplinary board. And, you roughed him up quite a bit, Lew. We can't have you on the team and now we have to send you back to Philly." Lewis' coach lowered his head as we spoke.

"No," Lewis insisted, "I can't go back to Philly! I can't go back; my dream is to play in the NBA!"

"I'm sorry, Lew."

Just like that, Lewis had lost his basketball scholarship and was destined to be on his way back to Philly. But he was scared to return; what would he tell his mother? He called a few friends he had made in Montana and stayed with them for almost a month and a half. Then, decided to go back and where he would finally face his mother and tell her what had occurred. After he had shared the news with her, he reached out to Mr. Sonny Hill for help. The NBA was the endgame and there was no way Lewis was giving up.

Mr. Hill had heard about the bit of trouble he ran into in Wyoming. Lewis explained the situation to Mr. Hill and how his heart was simply to protect himself from these malicious group of young guys. After a long and detailed conversation, Mr. Hill told Lewis he would think of what to do. Later that week, one of Mr. Hill's friends paid Lew a visit and offered to help. He offered to send him to a school in Lynchburg, Virginia to play college basketball there. Though Lew was unsure and unfamiliar with Lynchburg, this was his opportunity to keep playing basketball and continue his dream of going pro.

Two month later, when Lewis arrived in Lynchburg, he stood in front of three large buildings with a shred of confusion on his face. It was a seminary school with only approximately 100 students and no basketball team in sight. One of the administrative staff had suggested Lew attend Lynchburg college part-time in order to play but their team was filled. They had no interest in taking on any more players. One of the young men who had gone down to the college with him suggested they start their own basketball team in the seminary school playing against other local seminar schools. The gyms were smaller, and the crowds matched their size, but Lew was grateful to just play. Still, in his heart, it wasn't the same. He loved the noise of large crowds; he thrived in the performance.

After a year, Lew went to the school's librarian, Mrs. Peterson, and enlisted her help.

"I need to go to another college. I have dreams of going to the NBA. Can you please help me?" Lewis said.

Mrs. Peterson looked at the desperation on his face, "Lewie, your grades are pretty good. I'll tell you what, come back in a week and we will write letters to all the colleges down here, especially the African American Colleges."

Lewis was excited and also shocked; he had never heard of African American colleges. But the very thought breathed hope into his heart and his dream. Together, Mrs. Peterson and Lewis had written letters to several colleges. After a few weeks, he had finally started hearing back from the schools. But every school would offer partial scholarships. Financially, it just didn't work for Lewis. Then, to his surprise, Lewis received a letter from Cheyney State College. In the letter, he had found out that the head coach for their basketball team was John Chaney and they were offering him a full scholarship with room and board. It was January when Lewis packed his bags and made his way to back to Pennsylvania.

He drove for 8 straight hours, unable to contain the excitement. When he, finally, arrived at his destination; he met with the school's athletic director. Lewis shook Mr. Dave's hand and said, "I'm here now and I'm ready to play ball."

Coach Chaney, who was with Mr. Dave, told Lewis they had been looking for him since September. They already had their players for this season and there weren't any open positions. But they were looking forward to seeing him keep his grades up for an opportunity to try out next season. For Lewis, it was worth the wait. When tryouts started for the new season, he was ready. He gave it everything he had and made the varsity team! One again, Lew was playing in large gyms and for large crowds. Coach Chaney had given him the chance to be in the starting lineup and Lew did not disappoint. He had a great scoring record and loved to put on a show for the fans. It was especially great because he was from Philly, so many of them knew and supported him. Then, it happened, as if someone had thrown a large brick into a glass house and destroyed everything. Lewis had suffered an injury, one that would change his life forever.

Chapter 8

The vision that Lewis had for his future quickly changed during his senior year of Cheyney State College. Every dream he had of becoming a professional basketball player came to a halt. He was playing for the legendary Hall of Famer John Chaney and his last game was the best one he had played in the season. But as he was preparing to play for the state tournament, he broke his hand during that last practice. He was devastated when the realization dawned on him that his collegiate basketball career was over.

When he returned to college in the Fall semester, he felt lost. He was no longer a part of the varsity basketball team and things just weren't the same. He wasn't quite sure how to be a regular college student without being part of a team, after all, basketball had been a part of his life since he was thirteen years old. It was hard to decipher who he was without the sport that had brought him this far and given him the opportunity to attend college.

"Hey Lewy!" People would call out to him in the halls of the college, "I can't wait 'til y'all play this year! I'd love to come out to see you play! I love that shakin' bacon pull up jump shot you got and that charisma you got with the crowd!" Lewis loved that, he loved the atmosphere, the walking around the college, knowing he was a varsity basketball player. It meant a lot to him. But everything had changed. When he was no longer able to play varsity basketball, knowing he would never play college ball again, he began to feel abandoned. It was a very troublesome feeling at times.

One day he took a walk around the campus, attempting to fill the extra time he had on his hands. He came to a stop in the middle of the woods and looked up at the sky with tears in his eyes. "What should I do now God?" He choked out, searching the heavens for an answer. He stood there for a moment, just watching the different shades of blue and white with hints of pink. A calm settled on him shortly after and he suddenly knew the answer. It was as if God had come down from on high Himself and told him what his new passion in life should be. He needed to help kids like himself, who didn't grow up with a lot, form and actualize their dreams. Lewis spent just a moment wondering how he would do this, when he felt the answer in his heart: God would show him the way. His tears ceased to fall, and his resolve strengthened as he made his way back to his dorm room and prepared for classes as a normal student and not an athlete.

A few days later he ventured to the small town of West Chester which was close to his college. As he approached the local YMCA and saw the large number of children playing basketball and shooting pool, he decided this was where he should begin work for his new path. He started volunteering there regularly, teaching kids how to play basketball and talking to them about their futures. Not only did this help the kids, but it helped Lewis keep moving forward and occupy both his time and his mind. He knew that the best thing for him was to get out of the dorm rooms as much as possible and keep his mind occupied.

One particular day, a couple of his friends asked him to join them in their volunteer work giving out political information in their hometown of Chester, Pennsylvania. He agreed to join his classmates, so they made the trek from Cheyney University over to Chester. Once they all arrived in their hometown, Lewis met Mr. And Mrs. Jones who were community advocates for Chester city. They enjoyed helping the poor and the at-risk youth, and the community as a whole. Lewis soon came to find that his friends were part of Mr. and Mrs. Jones's youth club called The Young Black Society of Chester, a club dedicated to helping the community in any way possible.

They spent that day handing out flyers to help their political leaders both within their own city and in the surrounding county. Mr. and Mrs. Jones ensured that each volunteer was fed a delicious meal of fried chicken, collard greens, baked macaroni, hot biscuits, cake, and pie - all manner of good home cooking. Lewis had volunteered before at the YMCA in West Chester and they had given him a pretzel and canned soda. He had also volunteered at the Boys Club in Media, PA; and they had given him a hot dog and soda. So, this program in Chester was truly a treat for Lewis.

"Oh, my goodness," Lewis muttered to himself as the smells brought him back to his Grandmother's kitchen, "I have to come back here and volunteer again! This is way better than the college campus food! This is a real Southern, home-cooked meal right here!" He fell in love with volunteering for that group based on the food alone, not even taking into consideration, at first, that his new goal in life was to help those who started out as he did. At the end of the day he was asked if he wanted to join the group and be a part of this club that was devoted to helping the community do whatever was necessary for a better life for their youth. Without much thought at all Lewis agreed, thinking to himself that maybe God had directed him right to these wonderful people, so that he could fulfill the new vision he had for his life.

Lewis stopped going to college fulltime, he started working and taking a class here and there, while also spending a significant amount of time volunteering with the Young Black Society in Chester. In the summer of 1974, after school was over, he stayed on campus, working as a security guard with the university. This allowed him to live on campus. After work, one day, he went into Philadelphia and tried out for the professional summer league; sponsored, coordinated, and owned by Mr. Sonny Hill. They played at McGonigal Hall and had professional basketball games at night. He made it onto the PSFS professional team and played against both NBA and ABA players. He was getting off the bench and seeing some time on the court- maybe three or four minutes each game.

"Lewie, you're before your time!" His coach had told him one day, after pulling him aside.

"Why you say that coach?" He asked.

"Because you never stop running! You're up and down the court, you're doing your tempo and you're doing my plays but most of the time you're speeding up and down the court."

"It's only because I'm light on my feet coach! I can do anything and everything you want me to coach, but sometimes I just gotta keep moving." Lewis used to speed the ball down the court when he had the chance and come back around to set the play up; he was in control. At the time, the philosophy to professional league games was to walk the ball down the court, a slowed down tempo, with lots of hand checking. He didn't mind going side to side and stutter stepping as he brought the ball down, but he really enjoyed speeding down the court, moving fast and coming back around to score. He didn't mess with the coach's philosophy; he just was told he was too energetic and before his time.

Basketball meant a lot to Lewis, especially when he got to make a steal or assist when he was playing with the real professionals. He really felt that he was on his way to being in the NBA.

However, after the summer professional league was over, reality soon began to set in. He tried out for the Allentown Jets, a semi-pro team in the Eastern league. He made it onto the team and was getting paid around $325 a game, with a game Friday and Saturday nights along with practices. With the money he got paid he had to rent a car, pay for the motel room Friday and Saturday nights and by the time he had the chance to look around he only had about fifteen to twenty-five dollars left. Not only was this a huge disappointment to him, but during games he was getting less and less time on the court, only seeing about two, maybe three minutes of game time - on a good day. He put overtime in during practice, but he still wasn't seeing more time in game. He began to get disgusted with it all, but he didn't talk to anyone about it. His love of the game wouldn't allow him to walk away. He just kept showing up and waited for his name to be called because he loved the game so much.

His coach kept telling him he was doing really well during practices, but his time on the court during games didn't increase. Lewis never said anything to his coach, his dream of playing in the NBA was gradually fading. On top of that, the U.S. market for basketball players wasn't open, and they weren't playing abroad in those times. Lew, who knew nothing about the industry, didn't have an agent or anyone to help him navigate through the profession. Between playing semi-pro, attending college part-time, and volunteering; he had a lot on his plate. He was discouraged and frustrated. Eventually, he had had enough and stopped showing up at the games. He had given up playing semi-pro and had officially given up on his dreams of being in the NBA, although he was far from dreamless. He never stopped volunteering in Chester and soon enough his dream of being in the NBA was replaced by the faces of the little kids there that had no dreams. He sat down with them one day in the office and asked, "What kind of dream do you have to become a professional?" he asked them, wanting to know how to better help them succeed in life.

"Coach Lew...we don't have no dreams." One of them said softly.

"Well, if you come back, we're going to make a dream. We're going to find out what you can become." He promised as his new dream fully took hold in his heart. He wanted to help each kid find their dream and go after it. He dedicated himself entirely to this new dream, this thing he loved to do - helping someone else find their dream.

He approached Mr. and Mrs. Jones and told them that he had lost his dreams of playing in the NBA, but this opened up a desire to help kids find their dreams. He was committed to helping the organization grow, no matter what. He would ensure that what happened to him would never again happen to any other kid, as long as he could help it.

Lewis' dreams of playing in the NBA ended

Chapter 9

Lewis's new dream slowly came to fruition as he practiced Non-Traditional Social Work. He continued to work in his free time, volunteering for the local YMCA and his group of friends and colleagues in The Young Black Society in Chester. He was determined to help every kid find a dream, going beyond helping them with homework and finding jobs. The more Lewis worked with the society the more he got to know Mr. and Mrs. Jones. For instance, they lived directly across from the William Penn projects, so most of the children they helped were from those projects.

Their home was open 24/7, there were always kids who would spend the night in the Jones' home. It was incredible how they opened up their home, even though they had five children of their own and Mrs. Jones' parents lived there as well. Mr. and Mrs. Jones always told Lewis he was welcome to stay over should he need to, though he rarely accepted. He learned as the months went by that Mr. Jones worked full time for the Philadelphia Electric Company and that Mrs. Jones worked at the childcare agency. At that time, she had already devoted the last thirty years of her life to serving and helping the people of Chester- particularly the youth. She was the Founder and Executive Director of the program. And, Mr. Jones was always right there at her side, supporting her ambition and desire to help the people of their beloved city. Lewis learned that Mrs. Jones loved to brainstorm with the members of The Young Black Society, especially when it came to the idea to turn their society into a non-profit organization.

Her idea for the non-profit organization involved opening a store front office to hold services for the youth at risk within their town. There, they helped the youth after school with their school assignments. Together the society came up with the name Youth in Action for this new non-profit organization. The organization began to take off right around the time Lewis's dream of playing in the NBA finally died. He confided in Mr. and

Mrs. Jones in telling them he didn't have the funds to travel back and forth from the college to Chester. He told them he wanted to fully invest himself in his new dream of helping kids like himself, but he could only get to Chester occasionally while still going to school. One day shortly after, Mrs. Jones pulled Lewis aside and told him that Mr. Jones had been working on getting him a job in the city with the recreation department, which he had finally been able to do.

Lewis started working with the city of Chester in the evenings while going to school part time during the day. He worked hard and made it his mission to develop the city's recreational program while also expanding the basketball team that The Young Black Society founded. There were roughly 45 kids from the William Penn projects making up different teams in their club and Lewis worked with them all, hoping to keep them from going down the wrong path. Soon he was even able to find an apartment in Media Pennsylvania that was right by the R3 train station. The R3 train line seemed designed for him at the time, with stops in Chester, Cheyney State University, Media and Philadelphia- essentially all the places he needed to get to. Now he was able to commute from home, to school, visit his home in Philadelphia and get to Chester for work and help the Joneses develop their club into a Non-Profit.

Soon he was able to help Mrs. Jones receive the license required for them to open a storefront office and officially start the Youth in Action Non-Profit. They opened their office at 3rd and Kerlin Street in Chester, Pennsylvania and Lewis's dream truly began to take flight. The storefront was open from seven am until ten pm, Monday through Saturday. The first few years were all about service and collecting data. They began working on their track record of service so they could qualify for foundation grants from the state and county right away. After three years they had reached the continuing service requirements to qualify for funding and started getting bits and pieces of money.

There was so much Lewis was learning just from watching Mr. and Mrs. Jones work in the community and with the youth. Often. They'd work with juvenile delinquents and first offenders to overturn their cases and speak for them in court. During the 70's, there was an influx of young kids who would be found guilty on the charges brought against them and sent to Lima Detention Center. In many cases, the parents could not attend their hearing. So, either Lewis or Mrs. Jones would attend the hearings for these kids.

On one very memorable occasion, Lewis attended a hearing for a young teenage boy who had been wrongly accused. Since Lewis had been there many times before with Mrs. Jones, the judge knew him.

"Lew Fields," he called out. "See you're in here again. Are you the target?"

"No, your Honor. I'm here for this young man," Lewis replied.

"Anything to say here?"

"Your Honor, this young man was just in the wrong place at the wrong time. We really don't feel he should have to go to the Lima Detention Center." Lewis continued, "He plays basketball, he's a good student and has never gotten into any trouble before."

"Okay, I'll take that into consideration," the judge said. Afterwards, he called Lewis to his chambers and asked what should be done about this boy's situation. Lewis agreed to take the matter back to Mrs. Jones. This particular situation allowed Mrs. Jones to brainstorm with the community and together they formed a Restitution Program that would replace the option of going straight to the detention center. Instead, the youth would be given an opportunity to complete community service. This program gave way to breaking the cycle of stereotyping and making these kids believe that they were bad, and they were criminals. Most of them who entered the program, about 75% of them, never got in trouble again. Everyone makes mistakes and this program helped those teenagers get back on the right path.

Additionally, the club hosted weekly dances at the Armory, a basketball team in the winter and even some activities like roller skating- really just providing the community of Chester with whatever it took to help the people who lived there. One of their biggest projects was being the coordinator for the Summer Job Program of the city of Chester, funded by Delaware county from 1975-1977. They were in charge of helping 150-200 kids find summer jobs for three months every summer. When Mrs. Jones asked Lewis if he wanted to take charge of the program, he couldn't think of a reason to decline. So, every summer for three years in a row he searched for 200 kids who were able and willing to work and found them jobs throughout the city. It was frustrating at first, but eventually he got into the swing of things and got the kids jobs at community centers, hospitals, the YMCA, and even within the Youth in Action non-profit.

He helped to make sure that all the kids got to their jobs and if they didn't show up he followed up with them to see why, he made sure that their timesheets were filled out correctly and that they each got their paychecks from the summer job program. He had coordinators and program leaders working with him at the job sites and even set up a lunch program at each worksite so that he could be sure the kids would eat that day.

Communication with the children was very important to Lewis and he got to know not only the children but their families too. He talked to the kids in their programs, their brothers and sisters, moms and dads- sometimes it felt like there were at least a thousand families in the program, not just 200-300. He was working with mainly low-income families that were usually missing a parent, which made their involvement with Youth in Action all the more important. Mrs. Jones, in all her determination, was relentless when it came to helping these families. Should she find out that they had a problem, she would do anything in her power to attack it and fix it, if she could. Mrs. Jones never stopped helping the people of Chester, whether it was bringing business to the minority, continuing education work with the school districts, or feeding the poor, she was relentless. And she was an inspiration.

When they turned the club into a non-profit and started getting funds from the state Lewis was able to expand the basketball teams that they had originally and not only include more kids but also get everyone three-piece uniforms. With the help of sponsors, the Bell Telephone Company and Pepsi Company, he was able to include 300 children in a summer basketball league. He was able to create divisions in each project of Chester with different age groups- 13-15, 16-18, and an open division.

Soon, Lewis was able to turn the summer basketball league into the Collegiate Continuation Program, which would be the highest level basketball league in Chester, designed for young men who graduated high school and desired to play college basketball; but, due to their circumstances would never be afforded the opportunity. Lew wrote letters to the Athletic Directors of the surrounding colleges and universities. He petitioned to have his teams play against their freshmen teams, and they accepted. It was a 12-game season and the foundation provided transportation to these schools, uniforms, and other resources. Lew was overjoyed to provide these young men with the opportunity to play against schools like Lincoln University, Lehigh University, Georgetown, Cheyney, and others. The schools even set up college tours for his players. For Lewis, it was truly a remarkable experience. Several of his players went on to college and others went into the police academy. Lewis, himself, was blessed to have been offered a position at Lincoln University as the Assistant Head Coach of their Varsity Team. During his second year, he helped the Head Coach take the team to their 1st National Tournament in the history of Lincoln University.

Lewis was honored to do what he loved and serve in Youth in Action. As he grew in his role as an advocate and Assistant Executive Director, he was nominated for a panel largely recognized in the state of Pennsylvania. They were charged with traveling to Harrisburg and discussing policies that would help low-income families in the state. This panel was organized by Bob Woodson who worked alongside Mrs. Jones, often; they had been friends for over 15 years.

Youth in Action had outgrown their little store front. They were involved in so many community programs and activities, Mrs.

Jones turned to the faith-based community for help. Suddenly, the Youth in Action organization moved from a store front space to the educational building of the Trinity United Methodist Church on 9th Street.

Through Youth in Action, Lewis was finally realizing his dream of helping kids with theirs. He was an advocate for children like him, children that society would have otherwise written off, families that would have succumb to the labels of social class, and low-income communities that would have accepted the status quo. But everything he learned from the Joneses and every project he partook in within the organization, Lewis was just thankful to make a difference and be a part of it all.

The Pennsylvania House Grassroots Alliance Panel, representing organizations that serve low income citizens, meets monthly in Harrisburg to discuss legislation and issues such as job training and welfare reform.

Chapter 10

Lewis's CONTINUAL FAITH was tested at the passing of Mrs. Tommy Lee Jones, the founder and executive director of Youth in Action incorporated. By this time, Lewis was in his late forties. Mrs. Jones deemed him to be the co-founder of Youth in Action and it was his honor to serve in various aspects of the program. Lewis felt a sense of pride, joy and fulfillment working in the program as the Executive Director. All these years of gleaning from Mrs. Jones and advocating for the youth and the community – it all gave him a sense of purpose.

Twenty years had gone by and Mrs. Jones had confided in Lewis about her health. She wasn't sure what was wrong, but knew something was wrong, nonetheless. Where she once was an aggressive advocate for the community, she had now slowed her pace. Now, it was Lew who would travel to Philadelphia, Harrisburg, and Washington D.C. with proposals in hand. Lewis was in charge of getting contracts and meeting deadlines to receive funds that would sustain the program. Though Mrs. Jones' health changed, she never once complained or showed weakness. She was still very-much involved with brainstorming sessions for Youth in Action. She was still the life of the organization. So, when Mrs. Jones passed away, one night, the whole city of Chester felt the loss of the greatest community advocate that they had. The whole town grieved beside Lewis though this did little to comfort him.

His road through grief was painfully harsh and led to deep depression. Not only did he lose a wonderful role model and friend, but the organization also could not survive the departure of its fearless founder. And, so Lewis also lost the Non-Profit organization he had worked so hard to aide in developing. For with the passing of Mrs. Jones, Youth in Action was forced to close its doors as well. Shortly after, Lewis disappeared from Chester and, then, from life altogether.

When Lewis left Chester, he had moved to Sicklerville, New Jersey with his significant other. But Mrs. Jones' death caused

Lewis to spiral into such a profound state of depression that he lost his sense of purpose along with everything else. This had been the most devastating thing he had experienced in his life. Not even his dream of going to the NBA had affected him so badly. And, six months later, without having had the opportunity to recover from the loss of his dear mentor, his organization, and his purpose; Lewis lost his mother. The woman he loved most had passed away, and now things had taken a turn for the worst.

Lewis left all that he knew. He left his significant other and her daughter, and he barricaded himself in the streets of North Philadelphia surrounded by drugs and alcohol, attempting to numb the pain. Lewis was lost in a sea of hurt, loss, and confusion. Those on the streets who were around him looked after Lewis in their own way and as best they could, even with their own troubles. But, one evening, they all pulled together to take Lewis to the hospital, telling him that they didn't want him to die in those horrid streets. They wanted him to be well.

It was on that hospital bed that Lewis, with tears in his eyes, prayed to God. His words simple and heart-felt, 'Lord, save my soul and make me whole.' It was all he could muster, but that was all he needed. A few months later, his sister went to get him and take him to her house.

"Lewie, you are my brother. And, you are coming home with me," she said with compassion and grace in her eyes. Lewis, both speechless and grateful, packed his belongings and moved in with his sister. While living with his sister, Lewis continued to pray and ask God for healing and wholeness. As months turned into a year, he recovered and was able to go out in search for employment. Every day, Lewis went down to the career center to apply for job positions. One day, he received a response to an application for an overnight stock position at the Shop Rite in West Philly. He accepted the position and started his work. Soon, the change of pace and increase in activity had helped with his recovery. All the while, he had been keeping in touch with his significant other who was still living in Sicklerville, NJ. He called once a month, every month without fail.

A year later, while he was sweeping the grocery store parking lot, an African American man stepped out of his car and approached Lewis.

"Mr. Lew Fields? Is that you?"

"Yes...," Lewis answered as he turned around toward the man. It was one of the pastors of the faith-based initiative, Grassroots.

"What happened to you?" the young pastor proceeded to inquire.

Lew shared with the man all that had occurred from when he was in Youth in Action until now. The pastor invited him to his church at First African Baptist Church and Lew told him he would consider visiting. A few Sundays had passed before Lew decided to visit the church. The sermon topic, on that day, was that God is always with you, there for you; serve and ask for His assistance. It was as if God was speaking directly to Lewis. After service, the pastor went up to Lewis and greeted him. He asked Lew if he was still involved in sports, specifically basketball. He explained that he was on the board of the Christian YMCA and they were looking to put together a youth basketball team. Lewis was reluctant to help as it had been well over 12 years since he did anything involving basketball. Still, the pastor requested his help and guidance; and Lewis said he would think it over and get back to him.

A few days later, he reached back out to the pastor and spoke in detail about his overnight work schedule. The pastor told him they would make sure to plan around his schedule and give him a stipend for his work in coordinating the team. So, Lewis began working with the Christian YMCA to form their first ever youth basketball team. It was at this time that the buses went on strike and Lew was left without a means of transportation. His job at the grocery store was located over 70 blocks away from his home. For a week straight, Lewis walked to and from his job for his shifts. He was exhausted but persevered. This season of walking to work reminded him of the days in which he would train for basketball when he was younger. He thought about how he would run from South Philly to North Philly and back. Of course, now he was almost 50 and much had changed.

The basketball team program for the YMCA was a huge success. The program included kids from ages 8 to 12. Lew coached them in the game and counseled them with school and life situations. He encouraged the kids at every opportunity. God had used this project to life his spirit. This had given Lew hope.

Then, God sent him another connection. Lewis had an aunt named Virgue, who was his mother's closest friend, and she always told him she would never criticize him but rather support him in everything he did. One day, Lewis bumped into her son, Skip. They began to catch up, and Skip mentioned that he was working for the DRC Drug and Alcohol Center. He asked Lewis if he was interested in working there with him. With Skip's help, Lewis was able to get into the organization after he applied. Meanwhile, Lewis kept in touch with his significant other back in Sicklerville and her daughter. It had been 2 years, but he was faithful in making sure they were alright. Then, in one conversation, she asked Lewis if he wanted to come back home. All this time had passed, and he longed to be back with them, of course, his answer was yes. And, she made a promise that, if he returned home, she would help him continue to walk in his recovery.

So, Lewis continued to work at the grocery store and DRC, helping those with drug and alcohol addiction. Then, Lewis decided to go back to college and continue his education. Again, with Skip's help, Lewis applied and was accepted into the master's program at Lincoln University. But the road to his master's was anything but easy. First, Lewis went through their pre-master's session and, from there, continued to work on obtaining his master's which, ideally, would take 2 and a half years to complete. But the thought of returning to school after 20 years terrified Lewis and anxiety soon hit. His first semester proved to be a challenge; his grade point average was 3.1. However, to stay in the program, students must maintain a 3.0 GPA; and, if any of their classes fell below 3.0, they were required to repeat it. Lewis had ended the semester with one class below the required average. He was scheduled to retake the class.

The following semester only got harder with the additional class in his schedule. Coupled with his job at the grocery store, his work at DRC, and traveling from New Jersey to Philadelphia – it was too much for Lewis to bear. With each passing day, getting through the second semester got harder and harder. Eventually, something had to give, and Lewis did not return the following semester. Lewis quit three times during his journey toward his master's degree. It took him a total of nine years to finally complete the program. In 2009, with tears in his face and a sense of completion, Lewis walked down the aisle in his cap and gown to receive his degree.

Prior to their graduation ceremony, students were assigned to create a workshop in support of their thesis. Lewis' thesis was about providing empowerment for women on welfare, reforming working-class families, and fighting through the barriers within the welfare system, particularly in Chester. Lewis had organized a large workshop in the city of Chester with welfare workers in attendance. Many who also benefited from the programs of the Youth in Action organization also attended the workshop. That day, there were over 50 welfare recipients in attendance and over 20 welfare workers as well. The speakers in the workshop were three young former participants of the Youth in Action program. Remembering them in their teenage years coming to the program and seeing them now in their thirties, speaking before the crowd, brough Lewis to tears.

To witness the success of the workshop and its results was an emotional rollercoaster for Lewis. He was so choked up that when it was his turn to speak, he could hardly utter a word. Somehow, he managed to push through the tears and give his parting words.

"Do better. And, never give up. Do better for yourself, your families, and your children. If you do this; if you never give up, without a doubt, you will be successful."

Throughout his entire life, Lewis never gave up. And, as he reflected on all that he had lived through, as he contemplated on what would come next for him; Lewis was grateful for his perseverance and determination to help others. After graduation, Lewis kept working at his job and would often pray to God for guidance. His prayer was always, 'God, what can I do for You?' And, in one of those prayers, he received his answer, 'Continue helping someone else.' From then, he pledged that each day, whether he walked to work or rode the bus; he would find someone to help. It filled him up.

Lewis continued to work in the social services field, with ex-offenders, advocating on their behalf. If he walked into a Wawa to purchase a coffee, he was intentional about helping the homeless or those asking for money. He would buy them food and a beverage. Lew understood that it was the small acts that made a big difference. The younger generation would seek him out to talk to him, and he would bask in sharing advice and wisdom with them, encouraging them. He would make it a point to speak life into them and making it known that their lives had value. Regardless of who it was, if he saw a way to help someone, he did it.

Moving forward with his vision, it is Lewis' dream to use his experiences as an advocate for the people and walk in the role of a "non-traditional" social worker, to give those who want to go into the field of social work an in-depth feeling for that profession and an understanding of it should they choose to be a social worker. It is far deeper than a career, they must have a desire for it. It is his heart to speak to those in college who are studying to become social workers. You see, Lewis has seen the manifestation of changing people's lives through social work. Assisting someone to have a better life, showing love and appreciation for their lives; it is all a part of the field. For Lew, it was a calling. And, for those who want to walk in this profession, it should be as well. This is what Lewis learned most of all. And, as he walked in his purpose and calling for his life, he has tried to the best of his ability to follow the vision until the day God calls him home. This is the story of Lewis Fields, the non-traditional social worker, giver, and advocate for the people; but it is not the end of his story. For he will continue to pursue the spirit of goodness until the last day of his life, in which he will then hear from His Father in Heaven, "Job well done, my good and faithful servant."

About the Author

Lewis Fields MHS received his Master's degree from Lincoln University in Oxford, PA in 2009. Presently, Mr. Fields is employed at Gaudenzia DRC in the Intake/Admissions Department and has been there for the past 14 years. Fields was the Co-Founder of Youth in Action Inc, a non-profit community based social services agency. For over 20 years, he was also a community advocate for "at risk" youth and the low-income population throughout Pennsylvania, especially in Chester City, Delaware County. Fields has served on many city, county, and state committees during his tenure.

Lewis Fields played basketball on several levels including high school, college, and semi-professional. Fields also served as the assistant coach at Lincoln University in the early 1980's where his skills were instrumental in aiding the head coach and taking the team to the National Tournament for the first time in the school's history. The team at Lincoln University went on to be selected into the University Sports Hall of Fame. Throughout his life, Fields has impacted many young lives through basketball.

Today, Lewis Fields continues to seek out individuals whom he can help, his only form of payment is the fulfillment of his spiritual calling and the knowledge that he is doing God's will. Mr. Fields would like to hear from other "non-traditional" social workers, and those studying in the field, and their stories. You can reach him at ljfields08081@yahoo.com

Made in the USA
Columbia, SC
29 October 2020